The Sears Tower: The History of Chicago's Most Iconic Landmark

By Charles River Editors

About Charles River Editors

Charles River Editors provides superior editing and original writing services across the digital publishing industry, with the expertise to create digital content for publishers across a vast range of subject matter. In addition to providing original digital content for third party publishers, we also republish civilization's greatest literary works, bringing them to new generations of readers via ebooks.

Sign up here to receive updates about free books as we publish them, and visit Our Kindle Author Page to browse today's free promotions and our most recently published Kindle titles.

Introduction

The Sears Tower

"Chicago is a city of skyscrapers. New York is not. New York is a city that's a huge rock that has been carved out to make streets. [Gordon] Bunshaft was always jealous when he came to Chicago because he could stand and see the buildings. In New York, you can't do that. You have to be miles away to see the buildings." – Bruce Graham, architect

Walking around Chicago today, it's easy to forget about its past as a rural frontier, and that's due in no small part to the way Chicago responded to the Great Fire of 1871. Immediately after the fire, Chicago encouraged inhabitants and architects to build over the ruins, spurring creative architecture with elaborate designs, and architects descended upon the city for the opportunity to rebuild the area. Over the next few decades, Chicago had been rebuilt with the country's most modern architecture and monuments, and the Windy City's skyscrapers reached over 20 stories by the early 20th century, but it wouldn't take long for the city to turn its early skyscrapers into things of the past. Burnham's 22 story high Masonic Temple Building, once the tallest building in the world, was demolished in favor of buildings that were twice as tall.

The early skyscrapers that still stand look like antiques compared to Chicago's current skyline, because during the mid-20th century, architects built dozens of much taller buildings throughout Chicago, often constructing these enormous structures in less than a decade. In 1968, builders finished the John Hancock Center, the first building in Chicago to reach 100 stories, but Chicago's skyline gained its most iconic feature in 1973, the year the completed Sears Tower became the tallest building in the world.

Though it's technically named the Willis Tower today, Chicago's landmark is still best known as the Sears Tower, and Sears got a lot of bang for its buck. The Sears Tower only took two years to build at a cost of about $150 million, and it is still the second tallest building in America, a fact Chicagoans sharply debate after the Sears Tower was judged to be shorter than New York City's new Freedom Tower. In 1969, Sears wanted to create a large office space for its employees in the city, and they commissioned the firm Skidmore, Owings & Merrill to design and build the structure. The firm conceived of the now famous design, in which the first 50 stories of the structure were connected by what are essentially nine separate tube shaped buildings. After the 50th story, seven of the nine tubes rise up to the 90th floor. From there, only two tubes rise to the building's 108th floor. This design gives the Sears Tower the appearance of a large building at ground level that gradually tapers off into a thinner rectangle at the top.

Naturally, the size and shape of the Sears Tower have made it an inviting target for daredevils who like to climb skyscrapers and other tall structures. In 1981, Dan Goodwin used suction cups to help him climb the building and avoid authorities who tried to stop him. For added effect, Goodwin was wearing a Spider-Man suit. Even more impressively, in 1999 Frenchman Alain Robert climbed the building with his bare hands and climbing shoes. Of course, people looking for a safer way to the top can ride elevators to an observation deck on the 103rd floor, and over a million people choose this option each year.

The Sears Tower: The History of Chicago's Most Iconic Landmark chronicles the construction and history of the Windy City's most famous building. Along with pictures of important people, places, and events, you will learn about the Sears Tower like never before, in no time at all.

The Sears Tower: The History of Chicago's Most Iconic Landmark

About Charles River Editors

Introduction

Chapter 1: The Original Tower Design

"Sears, Roebuck and Company was incorporated in 1893 by Richard Warren Sears and Alvah Curtis Roebuck. In the years that followed, the small company grew tremendously, becoming the largest mail order business in the world by 1906. In the mid-1920s, Sears transitioned from the mail order business into regional stores. By 1969, Sears was the largest retailer in the nation, and looking to update their outdated headquarters. With a net income of $441 million that year, the company could financially support the development of an impressive modern building. However, Sears needed Chicago's support in order to make their move to the city center at South Wacker Drive. The company found support from Chicago's mayor, Richard Daley. He was keen on the commerce that Sears' headquarters would bring to the Chicago Loop area, which was partly undeveloped land. Daley also lifted the height restriction on buildings through a zoning ordinance revision in 1955; the ordinance changed the maximum building height to sixteen times the area of the lot. The only remaining obstacle to build higher was the Federal Aviation Administration, which set the maximum building height for Chicago at 2000 feet above sea level, or 1450 feet above ground. However, height did not initially concern Sears, as the original Tower design differed greatly from the final design." – Excerpt from a report made by the architectural firm of Skidmore, Owings and Merrill

1969 was a banner year for Sears, Roebuck & Co., whose retail stores and mail order catalog were American fixtures that allowed them to employ more than 350,000 people across the country. In fact, things were so good that Sears had a problem: they had outgrown their headquarters in Chicago and thus needed a new office space. Tired of having their people spread across the city, and with the resources to spare, the company decided to build something big enough to house everyone under one roof. According to architect Bruce Graham, who designed the Tower, "When the chairman—at that time Sears was different than it is now, it was strictly a marketing department and it did not have all the corporate things that it does now—the chairman wanted to build downtown. He first wanted to move out, those were the two choices, move out or build downtown. Mayor Daley and he made a deal, so he decided that he would move downtown."

Graham

Mayor Daley

Once they made that decision, Sears got in touch with Arnstein, Gluck, Weitzenfeld & Minow (AGWM), the company's long-time law firm, and at Sears' request, it set out to find a suitable site for the new building. After spending time evaluating the area and speaking with members of both the state and federal governments, AGWM returned to Sears with a couple of suggestions. After hearing them out, the Sears executives chose a two block lot in Chicago's Loop, at the corner of Franklin Street and Jackson Boulevard to the southeast and Wacker Drive and Adams Street to the northwest.

The first step was to get permission to close the portion of Quincy Street that ran through it, and when that was achieved, the firm sent Andrew Adsit to begin buying up the land they would need in the area. This was kept quiet, as word of their desire for the land would have definitely driven up the prices. Meanwhile, Sears hired the well-known architectural firm Skidmore, Owings & Merrill (SOM) to create a plan for the new building. Explaining that they would need at least 3 million square feet of office space, the mail order giant also expressed an interest in seeing how tall their new building could be. This caught SOM's attention and imagination, and they assigned high rise architect Bruce Graham to the project. As Graham later noted, "Chicago is a city of skyscrapers. New York is not. New York is a city that's a huge rock that has been carved out to make streets. [Gordon] Bunshaft was always jealous when he came to Chicago because he could stand and see the buildings. In New York, you can't do that. You have to be miles away to see the buildings. I was actually standing in front of the Empire State building with Roy Allen and a couple asked me where the Empire State building was. I said, 'You're standing right in front of it.' They didn't have any idea. You have no sense of the buildings. Rockefeller Center was the first one that you could see, and after that there were really none. Even Mies [Van Der Rohe] tried to do that by setting the Seagram back and then the architect next door took his building back, so it takes away from what Mies was trying to do which was to salvage a little plaza that was surrounded by buildings so that you could see the Seagram. So in Chicago, most buildings you can see. People love living in apartment buildings. They move there deliberately. In New York you can't help it. My son lives in New York and he can't help it, he's got to live in an apartment building. But in Chicago, people actually fight to see who's going to be over the twenty-first floor. You never build an apartment building less than twenty-one stories in Chicago, forget it. You can see the lake and the city and the airport."

One concern was that the building would need to fit into the Chicago cityscape and enhance it. Graham recalled, "The building that they had in mind was only sixty stories high, but with a massive floor. I told the chairman that if you ever move out of this building, nobody else is going to be able to occupy it and it will be a black cow in the middle of the city of Chicago. So he agreed. ... The old guys felt a responsibility to the city and the business community. ... The chairman did not want a monument. He said it may celebrate my employees and the city, but he was very clear, very emphatic about that. So it was not a solid monument. You feel the sense of space when you look at the Sears Tower, you feel that the structure is defining the floors and what have you."

Once permission was given, Graham enjoyed working with the people from Sears: "One of the things—the chairman's name, by the way, was Gordon Metcalf, and he was brilliant—Gordon said that he didn't want any of those damn diagonal things like the Hancock building. So by this time, I was working with Fazlur Khan on a lot of tube buildings, like the Shell Plaza building. It's very efficient, and costs a lot less than any of the New York skyscrapers, and you can build taller. We had built so many single tubes that I took out my cigarettes and I said to Faz, 'Why don't we build a whole bunch of little tubes that stop at different heights?' I had been thinking about it. And Faz said, 'That's a great idea!' So I built my cigarette structure and it worked. And it doesn't need diagonals because the structures go through.'

For his part, Metcalf remembered, "Being the largest retailer in the world, we thought we should have the largest headquarters in the world. But the genesis of the Sears Tower is more complicated than that. When the company decided to leave its sprawling old headquarters on Chicago's deteriorating West Side, height was the furthest thing from the executives' minds. They had bought a two-block plot on the western edge of Chicago's Loop and approached the problem of building the headquarters in exactly the same way as they planned any of Sears' stores throughout the world—from the inside out. The company began by studying its space needs, down to the number of desks for personnel. Then it projected its office requirements to the year 2003. Next, Sears hired the New York firm of Environetics to recheck the projections, draw floor plans, and figure out where every department should be located in relation to every other department. The result was… 'a building profile,' a jagged shape that looks like a child's random construction with wooden blocks of varying sizes. When this interior scheme was shown to…Bruce Graham…, he gasped: 'How do you expect me to design around that!'"

Graham ultimately presented Sears with a completely new design consisting of nine separate square "tubes," which were essentially nine separate buildings held together and covered by the same façade. These created a 225 foot square base that went up to the first 50 floors, and from there, the tubes at the southeast and northwest corners were capped off. The other seven tubes went up to the 66th floor, where the southwest and northeast tubes ended. Then, at the 90th floor, the three tubes on the north, south and east sides ended, allowing only the western and center tubes to go to the top of the 108th floor, making the final structure 1,450 feet tall.

In fact, it might have gone higher had the Federal Aviation Administration not stepped into to imposed limits for the sake of air safety. Graham later explained, "Originally there were more tubes, it wasn't just nine. The original design had six more tubes, so it was fifteen, a series of tubes going up and down. Harry Weese cried one night and said 'Bruce, I wish I had thought of that.' It was the best compliment I ever got from Harry Weese. We were in a bar under Wacker Drive. …I made the tube thing so that the top floors would accommodate smaller floors and I made the other floors smaller too so that they could be used by other users than Sears Roebuck."

Looking back on his most famous accomplishment, Graham noted, "The stepback geometry of the 110-story tower was developed in response to the interior space requirements of Sears, Roebuck and Company. The configuration incorporates the unusually large office floors necessary to Sears' operation along with a variety of smaller floors. The building plan consists of nine 75 x 75 foot column-free squares at the base. Floor sizes are then reduced by eliminating 75 x 75 foot increments at varying levels as the tower rises. A system of double-deck express elevators provides effective vertical transportation, carrying passengers to either of two skylobbies where transfer to single local elevators serving individual floors occurs."

With this design in place, it was time to let the world know of the plan, and the news hit the papers at the end of July 1970 like a thunderbolt. *The Daily Herald* in Utah informed readers in a headline that the "World's Tallest Building is Planned for Chicago," and the article reported, "Sears, Roebuck and Co. has announced it will build the tallest building in the world —200 feet taller than the Empire State building —in Chicago's loop. The new Sears building is to rise 1,450 feet from the street and house 16,500 persons, 7,000 of them Sears employees. It would be 100 feet taller than the World Trade Center, under construction in New York City, which is to be- 1,300-feet tall. New York's Empire State building, long the tallest in the world, will become the third tallest at 1,250 feet. The new building, named the Sears Tower, will be 109 stories high and have a gross area of more than 4.4 million square feet, spokesmen said. Gordon M. Metcalf, Sears chairman and chief executive officer, said the building is to be completed by 1974 and will be the company's national headquarters. Metcalf said the tower also will be the largest private office building in the world."

A few months later, the *Chicago Tribune* reported, "In order to assemble the property, Sears purchased 15 old buildings from 100 owners and paid $2.7 million to the city for the portion of Quincy Street which divided the property."

Needless to say, it would be money well spent.

Chapter 2: A Cost-Effective Solution

Pictures of the Sears Tower under construction

"It was only after Skidmore, Owings and Merrill (SOM), a structural engineering and architecture firm based in Chicago, got involved that the building took its final form. Sears performed several studies about the company's project growth and current business practices and concluded that their current and future space requirements were 2 and 4 million square feet, respectively, with a floor area of 110,000 square feet per department. Also looking for a cost-effective solution, Sears pictured a large 40-story cube. Instead, SOM determined by performing its own studies that departments could save significant amounts of time by stacking two 55,000 square ft stories on top of one another. This would change the building into an 80-story tower, but only if SOM could make it cost-effective." – Excerpt from a report made by the architectural firm of Skidmore, Owings and Merrill

Even as the foundation for the building was being dug, Sears was beginning to realize that it may have bitten off more than it could chew with the project. Scrambling to find a way to defray some of the costs of the building, the company decided to inhabit only part of the skyscraper so that the rest of the building could be rented out to other smaller companies. To this end, those in charge ordered Graham to add some attractive features, such as tall windows, to make the building more attractive to renters. Moreover, this arrangement would let Sears occupy more space as it was needed.

The second change that the company decided to make was to abandon plans to build a hotel next to the Sears Tower on the same lot. However, by the time Sears reached this conclusion, it was too late to correctly center the building on its lot. According to Graham, "that's why the building's on the side, they canceled it after we had already sited it. Then we had a link from which there would have been shops and then three more towers, but not that high, for the hotel. This is the tower, and this was to be the hotel. It was also to have had the penthouse, so this would not have been the same tower. ...it would have been south. That's why the building is oriented to the north. ...I almost cried because.... We would have sited it differently, but the building would have been the same. I don't really know what I would have done. I might have left the design so that you could add another office building to the south, but I'm not sure. But Sears Tower had the volume, the permissible volume to do it. They still do. They haven't used all the FAR, the floor to area ratio. ... The idea of reducing the floor, first, is that now it was usable by the smaller tenant than the big floors that Sears had. Then to reduce it, a lot of lawyers love it and they rented it all. Finally, the last piece went like this—the lower floors were designed so that you could take out a bay and the structure still goes through. You can take that out and take this out and have a U-shaped office floor with an atrium here and an atrium there. It's designed that way."

Another major concern on many people's minds was how such a tall building would hold up against Chicago's notoriously blustery environment. When asked about designing a building for the famously windy city, Graham was somewhat blasé about the process: "Tall buildings react to wind. ... It's not the highest by any means. Any city in the Midwest has a lot of wind. The winds from the sea are a lot higher than the winds in Chicago. The storms that went through [Florida] don't compare to the winds that went through Maine and Boston, those were really destructive. Chicago has had a one hundred and ten mile an hour wind at the Sears Tower, but that was way up on top. That wasn't really a problem. Stability is a concern. The fact that the Hancock and the Sears have a bigger base makes for stability. If you do the reverse, it's just the opposite of gravity. After a certain height, you have to start with a larger base, like the Eiffel Tower, with a narrow top and a large base."

Graham's peers at SOM agreed: "One of the greatest concerns for the bundled tube system was achieving sufficient lateral stiffness with an economic use of steel. The choice of steel likely stemmed from the building practices of the time, which used steel for tall buildings rather than concrete in Chicago. Though the Sears Tower is significantly taller than the John Hancock Center, the structural system uses a comparable quantity of steel per unit area. The closely spaced interior and exterior columns are tied at each floor with deep spandrel beams. At the truss levels, these tubes are tied together. These ties resulted in a stiffer structure, as the building acts as a unified system of stiffened tubes. The interaction between the individual tubes and the belt trusses at mechanical levels allows the building to attain its extreme height. These trusses serve an additional purpose beyond stiffening the tube structure against winds. Due to the drop offs, the gravity loading on the system is not evenly distributed along the height of the building. These trusses take the gravity loads from above and redistribute them evenly onto the tubes below. This is particularly important for the uppermost section of the tower, due to its asymmetry about the central axis of the building. Because the section is offset, its weight causes columns on one side of the building to experience a greater load than those on the other side. The presence of the belt trusses help to mitigate these effects of differential settlement, which cause the building to tilt. Though Khan had already estimated that the structure itself would save Sears a great deal of money, SOM continued to reduce costs for its client, as interest rates on the $175 million dollar project became higher and higher. In order to complete the project in a timely and economical manner, several new construction techniques were employed in order to fast track the construction."

Jeremy Atherton's picture of the John Hancock Center

A side view of the Sears Tower

One of Graham's biggest supporters throughout his career in general and on the Sear Tower project in particular was his wife Stephanie. In fact, she left her own unique stamp on the structure, as Graham himself later admitted: "My wife is a hell of an architect and she's my number one critic. Whenever I was doing something wrong, she was right. She liked Sears a lot. She ended up doing a lot of the interiors at Sears.

Graham, Kahn and the others also benefitted from the nature of the times in which they were working, as architectural historian Carol Willis pointed out: "And one saw that in other buildings of that particular moment -- of course in Chicago in the John Hancock Tower, or in the Sears Tower, which…was rising to become and take over the title of the world's tallest. But the principle that drove those buildings up and forward was a kind of implicit belief in the perfection of cooperation of architecture and engineering as a kind of aesthetic economy that balanced the kind of economics of the bottom line, that was so important in skyscraper design. One looks at the other buildings of that period, like the Sears Tower or John Hancock, and you see an American belief in technology, an ambition to build taller, to be better, to use technology to ascend. Whether it was to shoot for the moon and the space walks, or whether it was to raise the human and the radio and television antenna far above that -- to bring that technology to the top was a part of the belief in a sort of American invention and an advancing world where bigger is better, and technology solves problems rather than creates them."

An ironworker on the Sears Tower with the John Hancock Center in the background

A 1972 picture of a worker standing atop the antenna

Chapter 3: A Nuisance

"In cause 45199, the People of the State of Illinois ex rel. Jack Hoogasian and Julius Abler filed suit in the circuit court of Lake County to enjoin defendant from completing construction of its building in the city of Chicago. In cause 45216, the villages of Deerfield, Skokie and Northbrook and certain officials of Deerfield and Skokie, subsequently filed a similar suit in the circuit court of Cook County, charging that when completed the building would constitute a nuisance and that distortion of television reception would depress property values in the areas involved. Defendant's motion to dismiss the complaint for failure to state a cause of action was granted in the Lake County proceedings and appeal was taken. Thereafter, in the Cook County suit, a similar motion, which additionally averred that the action was now barred by res judicata as a result of the judgment of the circuit court of Lake County, was granted. Several plaintiffs in this action have appealed. We assumed jurisdiction of both appeals under Supreme Court Rule 302(b) and consolidated the causes for decision and opinion. On June 30, 1972, we entered an order affirming the judgments of the circuit courts, with an opinion to follow." - Justice Thomas E. Kluczynski of the Illinois Supreme Court

Kluczynski

Picture of the Sears Tower under construction

It should come as no surprise to anyone that there were unique challenges involved in building the tallest skyscraper in the world. While many of them had been faced by architects and builders in the past, at least one of the problems Sears ran into was unique to the latter half of the 20th Century. In March 1972, as construction of the building neared the halfway mark, the state's attorney in nearby Lake County filed suit against the company on behalf of "the People of the State of Illinois." According to the complaint, people were concerned that the new building would be so tall that it would cause problems with their television reception. In a story on March 24, the *Associated Press* reported, "Attorneys for two northern suburbs have indicated they will join the legal battle against construction of the Sears Tower building, a structure that critics claim will have an adverse effect on television reception for a half million viewers. The lawyers, Richard V. Houpt for Deerfield and Gilbert Gordon for Skokie, said Thursday they would file a joint complaint sometime next week in Cook County Circuit Court in an effort to stop construction of the gigantic structure. ... Other complaints have been filed against construction of the building claiming that 500,000 area residents living on a northwest-southeast line passing through the building's location would get 'ghosts' on their TV pictures. Critics say TV transmitters in the area would bounce their signals off the structure and viewers would see a double image, the second one from a reflected signal that takes longer to reach TV receivers. In addition to the complaint proposed by Houpt and Gordon, Lake County State's Attorney Jack Hoogasian has filed suit in Circuit Court at Waukegan seeking a delay in construction. Also, the Illinois Citizens Committee for Broadcasting has asked the Federal Communications Commission to take jurisdiction over the effects of the towers. Some critics feel home values will be lowered in affected areas, while others say that FM radio, especially stereo broadcasts, would be distorted. Sears has rejected an idea that the tower be lowered by 250 feet, a move some say would eliminate the ghosting problem."

As the suit worked its way through the courts, Sears racked up victories, even as each decision was appealed. Finally, the suit ended up before the Supreme Court of the State of Illinois. During this time, Sears offered space atop the completed building to television stations for use in broadcasting, but one newspaper complained that July, "Area television viewers can expect at least another year of reception difficulties on Channel 7 (WLS-TV). The ABC-owned and operated Chicago station plans to move its antenna from Marina Towers to atop the Sears Tower to alleviate 'ghosting' (double images) problems in the Northwest suburbs, but the move will not be made until fall of 1973. A spokesman for Channel 7 said yesterday 'We're all geared up to relocate' but structural reinforcement on the Sears Tower will take at least a year to complete. Sears, Roebuck and Co. offered Monday to help finance the relocation of all Chicago networks atop its 1,490-foot building. Northwest suburban residents began receiving double images, 'ghosting' on Channel 7 in March and the problem has become more severe. The station's officials say the construction of high-rise buildings, primarily the Standard Oil building, has obstructed the transmitting signal causing the interference. ... Originally Sears officials planned to install special absorbing materials on the Sears Tower to prevent interference to broadcaster transmitting from the Hancock Center. That solution however is inadequate, according to a Sears spokesman. The spokesman said the best solution to the 'ghosting' problems throughout the Chicago area is to relocate all stations atop the 100-story Sears Tower."

Others agreed with the idea, some of them even enthusiastically. The article continued, "The FAA has given final approval for a 350-foot extension to the height of the Sears Tower to allow the television antennas. Channel 7 officials and Channel 32 (WFLD-TV) were very pleased with the Sears announcement and indicated they hope to relocate the transmitters, other stations merely said they will study the proposal. ... Channel 26 (WCIU) transmits from the Board of Trade building and has indicated it wishes to move to the Sears Tower. ... Each station is expected to spend some $1 million to move to the Sears Tower. A Channel 7 official said the move from the smaller Marina City building to the towering Sears structure will 'give the crispest signal you have ever had in the Northwest suburbs.'"

Finally, on September 20, 1972, the judges issued the following decision affirming Sears' right to continue building: "The complaints basically alleged that defendant envisions the construction of a building in the city of Chicago which will reach a height of 110 stories or 1350 feet. At the approximate time of the filing of these actions the construction had progressed to a height of 50 stories. Plaintiffs alleged that if construction was allowed to continue the building would interfere with television reception in certain areas. This interference would occur because the broadcasting antennas of Chicago television stations are lower than the contemplated structure which would cause the signals that emanate from these antennas to abnormally reflect from defendant's building thereby allegedly producing distortions on television screens in these areas. The principal issue in this case is whether defendant has a legal right to use the air space above its property subject only to legislative limitation, or stated conversely, whether an individual or class of individuals has the right to limit the use of such property on the basis that interference with television reception constitutes an actionable nuisance. ... In effect we have competing legitimate commercial interests, both of concern to the public. ... The responsibility in this case for inadequate television reception in certain areas rests more with the broadcaster's choice of location than with the height of defendant's building. Therefore disruption of television signals initiated by totally independent third parties over which defendant has no control cannot be the basis for enjoining the full legal use and enjoyment of defendant's property...it is clear to us that absent legislation to the contrary, defendant has a proprietary right to construct a building to its desired height and that completion of the project would not constitute a nuisance under the circumstances of this case."

Chapter 4: Something Distinctive

"Fazlur Khan, the engineer selected to work on the project, came up with the structural system that defined the Sears Tower. This bundled tube system gave the building its physical strength while saving Sears $10 million as compared to pre-existing structural systems. Khan had already worked on another Chicago project, the John Hancock Center, with architect Bruce Graham. In that building, he had used another innovative structural system, the braced tube, which tapered towards the top to provide for various tenant requirements. As the building contained an excess 2 million square feet compared to the initial space demand, Sears needed to consider various tenant requirements, and the shape of the John Hancock Center was similar to what they needed. However, Sears and Graham both wanted something distinctive, not another 'Big John'. This required a new structural system." – Excerpt from a report made by the architectural firm of Skidmore, Owings and Merrill

Khan

Much of the credit for the Sears Tower's design goes to Fazlur Khan, who was instrumental in revolutionizing the construction of skyscrapers. As Stephen Bayley recently wrote in *The Daily Telegraph*, Khan invented a new way of building tall. [...] So Fazlur Khan created the unconventional skyscraper. Reversing the logic of the steel frame, he decided that the building's external envelope could – given enough trussing, framing and bracing – be the structure itself. This made buildings even lighter. The 'bundled tube' meant buildings no longer need be boxlike in appearance: they could become sculpture. Khan's amazing insight – he was name-checked by Obama in his Cairo University speech last year – changed both the economics and the morphology of supertall buildings. And it made Burj Khalifa possible: proportionately, Burj employs perhaps half the steel that conservatively supports the Empire State Building. [...] Burj Khalifa is the ultimate expression of his audacious, lightweight design philosophy."

The Burj Khalifa

While the popular engineer Khan was assigned to oversee construction, he had plenty of help from others. SOM explained, "The initial stages of design and construction went smoothly for the Sears Tower. As the design moved forward, Fazlur Khan was unable to spend his full time on the project, as he was a partner at SOM. Instead, the project team was composed of six to eight people at any time, with Hal Iyengar as the team leader. The structural drawings were fast tracked along with the construction schedule, taking only 3 months to complete, rather than 8 months. The project team worked overtime, using computer modeling in order to meet the deadline. Once the final design was completed, construction began with the foundations, and proceeded according to plan."

Iyengar

In the building industry, as in many other places in the world, time is money, and Sears wanted to save both. As such, the company insisted that its new corporate home be completed as soon as possible. SOM explained how that affected their work: "Due to the rapid construction process, prefabrication was one of the most important principles employed during the building of the Sears Tower. Structural units called 'Christmas trees' allowed for a 95% reduction in welding on the job site. The units were welded offsite and consisted of a two-story column with half-length beams welded to either side of the column. On site, the units only needed bolted splice plate connections between beams and web bolted connections for the column splices. As welding on site is one of the most costly and time consuming aspects of steel construction, this process saved a great deal of money for Sears. This use of prefabrication of the Sears Tower project significantly streamlined the construction process. The assembly process was also streamlined through the use of four standard S2-type stiff-legged derricks. These derricks were used to lift modular units of up to 45 tons up to the 90th floor construction. A final guy derrick was added on the 90th floor for construction up to the roof. For the entire construction process, the derricks were moved after four stories had been completed (two tiers of the prefabricated steel units). With this efficient use of machinery, the erection speed was typically eight stories a month. The steel construction assembly finished on time after 15 months. Overall, the construction of the Tower was mostly without incident, as the designers and contractors obviated most issues associated with super tall steel building design."

While the company and its engineering firm could set all the deadlines they wanted, the building project ultimately depended on the men and women doing the work at the site. On this subject, Graham was uncharacteristically enthusiastic, saying, "The Chicago workers were terrific. ... I think by and large the buildings I worked on in Chicago the workmen have loved. But Sears was a new experience and it was more for steelworkers and glaziers. It was, I believe, the tallest steel structure in the world. ... Steelworkers are wonderful. They have to start from the ground, because if you start them on the tenth floor, they'll fall off. I'll never forget the great topping-off ceremony when the last piece of steel went in. Mayor Richard J. Daley was there and the police came and said to us, 'The steelworkers are out there making a riot. What should we do, Mayor?' And he said, 'Leave them alone!' I agreed with him. Steelworkers are just unbelievable workers. Believe it or not, they're gentle. ... They were applauding as it went up each step of the way. ... The funniest thing about that was that we have photographs of the plumbing being set in place ahead of the steel. It was under construction as we kept going. They were prefabricating it and as soon as they could get the steel up there, it went right in. The workers were wonderful. I can't tell you how much I admired Chicago construction workers."

When asked about working with the infamous Chicago unions, Graham was equally praiseworthy: "Without the unions, those workers wouldn't be any good. They wouldn't make any money. It's a problem for the chairman of General Motors, but it's not a problem for the worker who gets paid to risk his life by walking on a steel structure. ... The best plasterer in the world, Monroe McNulty, worked in Chicago. ... I'd go to ask the plasterers how to do it. Come on, they know better. They'd have it all done in plaster, no drywall, in Chicago, by McNulty. You can't believe how accurate it was. We had some furniture made in New York by another craftsman for our living room in our home and they just set it in. The dimensions that McNulty put in the plaster were right on the button. ... My personal experience with Chicago construction workers was terrific in every sense. The union trained them. ... Who else trains them? If you think the schools on the South Side train them, they don't. They're trained by the union. Apprenticeship."

For a while, the project's major troubles were legal and financial, but in April 1973, there were a number of significant accidents at the site that called into question how safely the entire project was being run. On April 6, the *Chicago Tribune* reported, "Large scaffolding planks broke loose from the 108th floor of the Sears Tower yesterday and fell into Adams Street injuring two women. A window in the Fashion Trades building, 318 W. Adams St., was broken by a piece of the falling lumber. Janet Jaegers, 22, of 2711 N. Magnolia St., was hit by fragments of the planks and treated in Henrotin Hospital. She was later admitted to Grant Hospital in satisfactory condition. Louise Hogan, 61, of Rt. 4, Antioch, was treated at Henrotin Hospital and released after she, too, was hit by fragments. Both women were also struck by pieces of glass from windows broken by the falling planks. A spokesman for Sears, Roebuck and Company said the scaffolding was being used for interior construction work. He said it had somehow blown through a space where windows are to be inserted. The Sears tower is being constructed at Adams and Franklin Streets."

Just days later, on April 11, a fire suddenly swept through the building. According to one *United Press* story, "Four workmen were killed Wednesday when a flash fire shot through an elevator shaft between the 33rd and 42nd floors of the Sears Tower, which when completed in a month will be the world's tallest building. The dead were identified as Leonard Olsen, 44, Chicago; Robert Wiggins, 52, Park Ridge; William Walsh, 22, Melrose Park, and Larry Lucas, 20, Lincolnwood. 'When I heard the men screaming, I knew they would be dead because it has happened that way before on other jobs,' said Michael D. Michele, a carpenter working on the 30th floor of the tower. There apparently was no chance of escape for the victims because the marble lined shaft was what construction men call a "blind hatch," meaning it had no exit at the bottom. 'We heard screaming from the elevator shaft and about 30 men broke through the wall with sledge hammers,' Michele said. 'It took us about 20 minutes. When we reached them, I saw two charred bodies and a man who was still alive. But by the time they got him to the ground, he was dead.'"

An investigation quickly followed, and the *Associated Press* subsequently reported, "The four men were cleaning the elevator mechanisms with a solvent at the 42nd-floor level Wednesday when the fire broke out, Fire Chief Leo Kelly said. There is no exit from the elevator shaft at that level. Kelly said three of the men apparently jumped from the elevator platform to escape the intense heat. Their bodies were recovered at the bottom of the freight shaft on the 33rd floor. The fourth victim was found in the elevator cage at the point where the fire started. Kelly said the four men were using a bucket of cleaning solvent which workers said was not flammable. Flames suddenly swooped around the platform and raced down the shaft from the 42nd to 33rd floor. 'It was a flash fire that began in the elevator shaft, probably from an electric spark,' said relief Fire Marshal John E. Murray Jr. 'The exact cause is unknown.' An investigation to determine whether there were any safety violations that caused the fire was started by the Department of Labor's Occupational Safety and Health Administration. A sample of the cleaning solvent being used was undergoing analysis at the Chicago Fire Academy. The bodies of the four men were recovered by crews breaking through marble, steel and concrete walls with sledge hammers after trying to locate and reach the screaming men. 'We knew what was happening right away and we knew we had to break through the wall, explained Michael De Michele, 20, a carpenter. ... All four men were employees of the elevator division of the Westinghouse Electric Corp., a contractor on the Sears building. The shaft where the men were working was a 'blind shaft' running between the 33rd and 64th floors. It has only about 10 openings on floors. The deaths raised to five the number of workers killed on the $150-miillion skyscraper. An ironworker was killed last October when he fell off a beam and plunged four floors."

Later that month, another worker lost his life on the 105th floor. Anxious to avoid any more bad publicity, the company was able to keep the story pretty quiet; one article reported simply, "A workman fell to his death Saturday when he slipped on the 109th floor of the Sears Tower and fell 35 feet to a floor below." One of the reasons there was such little interest is that the story was quickly overshadowed by news of severe weather in the area. On April 20, 1973, the *Associated*

Press noted, "The National Weather Service recorded wind gusts of 55 miles per hour at Midway Airport and a sustained wind of 54 m.p.h. for about 45 minutes. In Chicago's downtown area, the streets around the Sears Tower, soon to be the world's tallest building; were closed as the winds popped out windows sending pieces of glass into the area."

Chapter 5: Naturally Informs Its Space

"For years the tallest building in the world, the 110-story Willis Tower (formerly Sears Tower) marked a major step toward exemplifying and defining SOM's belief that a building's structure should naturally informs its exterior profile. The tower's structure comprises nine squared tubes, each rigid within itself without internal supports. The tubes are bundled together as a closed square above the first 50 stories, and terminate at varying heights, creating a multi-tiered form. The structural steel frame was pre-assembled in sections and then bolted into place on site. The lightweight building skin, a black aluminum and bronze-tinted glare-reducing glass, serves as an insulator between the interior and exterior structure in order to maintain a relatively constant temperature, which minimizes the expansion and contraction of the frame. The 4.5-million-square-foot tower was the headquarters for Sears Roebuck & Co. from the time of its completion in 1973 until 1995, when the merchandiser relocated to suburban Chicago. The building's design, flexible floor plan, and iconic stature enabled it to become a premier address for a host of Chicago companies and firms. Today, the tower is well-maintained and remains a center of activity in Chicago's Loop." – Excerpt from a report made by the architectural firm of Skidmore, Owings and Merrill

The building was completed on May 4, 1973, and one publication described the scene: "A 2,500- pound carbon steel beam signed by hundreds of Sears Roebuck and Co. employees was hoisted more than a quarter of a mile into the air Thursday to top out the Sears Tower, officially making-the structure the world's tallest - The steel and glass super building on the southeastern section of Chicago's downtown area rises 1,454 feet 110 stories— and measures 4.5 million square feet [at its base.]"

Daniel Schwen's picture of the Sears Tower

Pete Stewart's photo of the Sears Tower

The day before, the *Chicago Tribune* had proudly announced "Today's the Day--Sears Tower Becomes Tallest of the Tall." The article reported, "With its topping out today, Chicago's Sears Tower will become the world's tallest building towering above other famous skyscrapers around the world. Ironworkers will bolt the last steel girder into place atop the 100-story, 1,454-foot structure today. More than 1,500 men have worked on the building since construction began in 1970. The building which is scheduled for completion next year, will provide more than 4.4 million square feet of office space and will have cost more than $150 million."

Sent to cover the topping out of the building, Robert Enstad wrote on May 4:

"A final 2,500-pound girder was lifted a quarter mile into the sky yesterday to make the Sears Tower the world's tallest building. It almost didn't come about. Strong winds threatened to delay the topping off of the building. It was feared the heavy beam would break some windows on its way to the top. But the strong, cold winds seemed to die down just long enough for the lifting as dignitaries below stretched their necks upward and a chorus of hard hat electrical workers sang these lyrics:

She towers so high
Just scraping the sky
She's The Tallest Rock."

Enstad confirmed their estimate: "She is indeed the tallest rock as she pierces the clouds 1,454 feet [nowadays over 1,700 feet] above Wacker Drive at Jackson Boulevard. A frame of 76,000 tons of steel encloses 4.5 million feet of floor space. Richard Sears could never have dreamed of such an edifice bearing his name when he brought his fledgling mail-order business to Chicago in 1887. Yet there she stood in the clear but cold sky yesterday as a monument to what is now the world's largest retailer--Sears Roebuck & Co.--and man's ability to reach higher and higher in search of a place to work and live. 'I want to thank them [Sears] for staying in Chicago when so many are leaving,' said Mayor Daley. 'Sears Roebuck, a name that means everything to the people of America, has no equal in the business world of Chicago.' 'We ask that each time we look at this tower, may we be reminded of our unity,' said Cardinal Cody. Gordon Metcalf, retired chairman of the board of Sears, told the dignitaries who sat shivering in 42-degree temperatures fanned by strong north winds that Sears Tower almost wasn't the biggest. He said twin towers, which would not have been as high as the new tower, were considered for the three-acre site. … A few minutes later a group calling themselves the Tower Bums started singing 'The Tallest Rock,' a sort of folk-rock composition, and the white beam with 12,000 signatures on it began its final journey to the 110th floor."

Of course, no one could have the special sense of pride shared by those who had actually helped build the new skyscraper. According to Enstad, "It was a great moment for both Sears and the Tower Bums, a group consisting of Bob Rameke, John Meyer, Jack Gallagher, and Howard Nowotarski. All have been electrical workers at Sears Tower. Rameke composed 'The Tallest Rock' for yesterday's occasion. As the last beam went into place workmen already were putting in carpeting and installing cabinets in the lower floors of the Tower, whose present stage of maturity depends on what floor you are on. The beams are now all in place. The concrete flooring is completed to the 101st floor, and aluminum and glass windows are in up to the 88th floor. Occupancy of the building will begin late this year. Completion is not expected until next year. At that time Chicagons (sic) will have a chance to see how Chicago looks from a public observatory on the 103rd floor."

Views of Chicago from the 103rd floor observation deck

Olga Bandelowa's picture from the observation deck's glass balcony

Harkening back to the controversy over the television reception, reporter Kurt Baer wrote, "The Sears Tower was topped a 1,454 feet yesterday, and an engineer at Channel 7 (WLS-TV) said the station hopes to be broadcasting a signal from the top of the world's tallest building by December. Installing new broadcast equipment atop the tower is expected to end reception problems on Channel 7 experienced by area viewers. Channel 7 now broadcasts from the much smaller Marina City building and the recent construction of the Sears Tower. the Standard Oil Building and other super skyscrapers have been interfering with signal reception throughout the metropolitan area* Northwest suburban residents first began noticing "ghosting" (double image) problems about a year ago when the Sears Tower was a mere 66 stories high. Yesterday, the last structural beam in the building was hoisted 110 stories to the top. IVAN WRABLICK, an engineer with Channel 7, said the station is in the process of ordering over a million dollars' worth of news broadcast equipment to install in the Sears building at Wacker Drive and Adams. "Sometime in December we hope to be broadcasting with an interim antenna which we will use until main antennas are installed in the building," he said. The new equipment should clear up broadcasting problems in the Northwest as well as other parts of the metropolitan area where reception has not been good, Wrablick said."

The article then went on to detail what had been done to ready the building for its new tenants:

"Sears spokesman Ernie Arms said yesterday mounts for permanent antennas already have been built on the tower's 85th floor and that a temporary tower for Channels 7 and 11 will be installed this fall. Installation of permanent antennas will await decisions from other broadcast companies which, Arms said, are now studying the cost and desirability of moving to the Sears Tower. Channels 7 and 11 have had the most serious reception problems, along with Channel 26 which plans to move to the Hancock Center. Channel 11 now broadcasts from atop a high-rise apartment building at 1000 Lake Shore Dr. According to Wrablick, there will be little if any noticeable difference between the picture put out from the temporary antenna and that broadcast from the permanent facility. The temporary tower will extend 85 feet above the main roof of the Sears Tower which is at the 109th story. The top floor in the building is a "penthouse" where mechanical and electrical equipment will be stored. Television towers were not originally part of the Sears Tower design and locating the broadcast antennas on the building necessitated special strengthening of the structure. The Federal Aviation Administration also had to approve a height variation for the tower. The Sears Tower has 4.5 million square feet of office space and will be the workday home for some 15,000 employees, of which approximately 7,000 will work for Sears."

Chapter 6: Standing Tall, Proud, and Respectful

"Viewed from afar, the Willis Tower integrates into the Chicago skyline, standing tall, proud, and respectful. The overall style of the building, with its simple black facade stressing verticality, reflects the prevalence of Miesian architecture in Downtown Chicago. From a distance, the simplicity helps demonstrate the structural system, as the lack of decoration instead features the tubular construction. The intersecting column lines are also abundantly clear, even from several miles away, adding to the visual separation of individual tubes. Black louvres cover the trussed levels of the building, making these levels apparent and visually clean. The Willis Tower has been a part of the Chicago skyline for nearly 40 years. The exterior building material shows very little aging, a sign of its durable construction. Not only has the skyscraper become an integral part of Chicago's skyline, many of its details have allowed it to remain an effective and modern symbol of downtown Chicago." – Excerpt from a report made by the architectural firm of Skidmore, Owings and Merrill

Once the building was opened, the reviews began to pour in. Paul Gapp, an architecture critic for the *Chicago Tribune*, wrote in February 1974, "Any plea to call a halt to gigantism is futile. We are stuck with it and we are going to get more of it. We can only hope that those colossal urban growths are created with at least as much skill and sensitivity as that which resulted in Sears Tower...In the end, what we have here is a building whose exterior profiles are a bold, vital, and exciting departure from orthodox mediocrity; in sum, a finely engineered piece of sculpture, even if its interior is largely nondescript...Let us give thanks that Sears' request for 4.5 million square feet of space was not fulfilled by someone who decided the solution was to build the world's largest cracker box."

Some years later, Blair Kamin wrote in *Why Architecture Matters: Lessons From Chicago*, "Since its completion in 1974, Sears has failed to capture the popular imagination the same way as the 102-story Empire State, whose robust setbacks and powerfully sculpted mooring mast were made to order for the celluloid climbing exploits of King Kong. Nor has Sears become a beloved urban icon in the manner of the 100-story John Hancock Center, whose bold X-braces and tapering profile lend it a skyline swagger that perfectly captures Chicago's broad-shouldered image of itself. Sears, in short, is more a triumph of engineering than of architecture, a building that is admired more for achieving great heights than for its ability to translate its structural bravura into sky-high drama."

Not only did the reviews pour in, so did the tourists, who flocked to the building in droves. This led to some unintended consequences and a call from Sears for Graham to come back and make some changes. He later explained, "I did the first addition and the first change, but it was very simple. The reason for the change was that the building was more popular than we thought. So the people going to the observation deck were bustling through the office users, so the change was made to make it easier to separate that traffic. [The barrel vault entrance is] the beginning of the separation. And also the front was slightly changed so we could make that separation from the front. We were trying to get most of the people who go to the building for office work to come in on Jackson. … It was an admission of a huge success that we never thought would happen. The fact that there was the Hancock made it even more so, not less so. The kids go up at the same time and watch one another and talk to one another. They'd go up there when there was lightning and it was packed. It's a great show. You'd see the antennae lightning up and go 'Crash!'"

Graham's work on the changes refined his perspective on architecture and led him to muse, "An office building—any urban building, especially hospitals, by the way—should be like a loft building, because the changes in society change the use. So Sears is an ideal example because I could take the floors out, I could make it higher or lower, that is important when you're building in the city, because it's not so easily taken down. It's an investment, not only of Sears, but of the city of Chicago. It's an investment of the city itself to allow this building to be built, so that it could be used for anything. I could have put apartments in the Sears Tower, it would have taken less elevators, by the way. I could have put a factory in it, because office buildings are really factories. I'm convinced now that we don't need to have dropped ceilings in an office building. Every office building and technical building should have a raised floor, not a false ceiling. Because with computers and computer technology, you don't want the light coming from there. You can't read them. You want the light to be very low from the ceiling and all power and light to be around the equipment. Think of it as a factory. I can make the Sears Tower into a commercial and industrial factory, no problem. That is important, as opposed to the sadness of the old Sears building on State Street that can't support the weight of a library."

Almost a decade later, the Sears Tower was remodeled again. *The Chicago Tribune* reported on November 14, 1983, "Sears, Roebuck & Co. has awarded two contracts for a $20 million-to-$30 million renovation of all the lower-level public space in Sears Tower--150,000 to 200,000-square-feet. The contracts for the job went to the same companies that did the original design and structural work on Sears Tower: architects and designers Skidmore, Owings & Merrill and contractor Morse-Diesel Inc. Sears Tower, which opened in 1974 with its 110 stories and 4.5 million total square feet, is renowned as the tallest and one of the two largest buildings in the world. Its lower-level space, however, has earned the more dubious distinction of being confusing to people who frequent the building as well as to the uninitiated pedestrian. Skidmore referred questions about the project to Sears. Morse-Diesel Assistant Vice President William Lyons informed his firm had won the contract, but he said Sears would have to fill in the details. Sears Spokesman Ernie Arms said, 'We're several weeks away from an announcement. No details are available yet.' Sources say Skidmore beat out architects John and Norman Schlossman, and Charles Kober Associates, and that Morese-Diesel won the contract over Schal Associates Inc. One of the project's features, sources say, is a new atrium entrance off Wacker Drive that will extend from the sidewalk to the present doorways. In addition, plans call for an overall 'opening-up of space.' The project may slightly raise the rents in an already high-rent district, but it's believed to be intended to spruce up the image of Sears and its tower. Some also theorize the renovation may be a testimonial to Chairman Edward Telling, the man who directed Sears' metamorphosis from a sluggish retailer into an aggressive financial services giant. Guesses vary as to why Sears rejoined forces with Skidmore, which designed the confusing public space area to begin with, but one industry executive comments: 'You married? Well, you have fights and disagreements, but you get back together again. It's comfortable.'"

Regardless of others' opinions about the changes made to the Tower, Graham was unhappy with the new developments: "Ada Louise Huxtable came to visit it before they made the changes on it—because the remodeling that has been done is anti my ideas—she said it was the only democratic high rise building she ever saw. And it was. It was very simple, there were no big stainless steel interiors. There were white plastic elevators. And the building was very simple. And who was the sculptor? Sandy Calder. What have they done now? They've changed the lobby and made the ceiling higher and they changed the proportions of the Calder. They're animals." On another occasion he complained, "It changed the whole idea that the black columns inside reminded you of the black columns outside, right? I wanted to give the sense of time, to recognize that this black column is like that black column and that you're moving through a space between them. It was terrible. [Jim Stefano] did the elevators, too. ... John Buck was the one who hired him at the time and I can't stand John Buck. He was representing [the building], I don't know exactly what his role was."

Nonetheless, in describing the Sears Tower today, SOM wrote that the building "consists of a structural steel frame that was pre-assembled in sections and then bolted in place on the site. The lightweight building skin — a black aluminum and bronze-tinted glare-reducing glass curtain wall — serves as an insulator between the interior and exterior structure to maintain a relatively constant temperature, in turn minimizing the expansion and contraction of the frame. Structurally, the building pioneered the use of bundled tube construction. The tower is composed of nine bundled structural tubes resting on reinforced concrete caissons that go down to bedrock. The caissons are tied together by a reinforced concrete mat. The iconic setback design of the structure was conceived as a direct result of the client's space requirements. The designers were required to develop a building that incorporated not only very large office floors, which were necessary for the company's operations, but also a variety of smaller floors for tenants requiring less floor area. The basic structure developed for this program of the tower consists of nine 75-foot-by-75-foot column-free square tubes at the base, forming a cellular-tube frame. Floor sizes were reduced by eliminating 75-foot-by-75-foot increments at varying levels."

According to SOM, the Sears Tower "draws its strength, both visual and physical, from its structural form, the bundled tube. The building plan consists of 9 squares, each 75 feet across, placed in a three-by-three grid arrangement. Each square has 5 columns per side spaced 15 feet on centers, with adjacent squares sharing columns. As the columns rise up the building, each square in the plan forms a tube, which can be seen on the exterior of the building. These tubes are independently strong but are further strengthened by the interactions between each other through truss connections. While the tubes connect at each floor level with beams and floors trusses, several large trussed levels act as the main horizontal connectors in the buildings. These trussed levels, which also contain the mechanical systems for the building, appear as black horizontal bands on the façade. While the louvres covering the trussed levels mask the structural details, the purpose of these levels remains abundantly clear visually."

Chapter 7: Big Willie

"Chicago natives now affectionately call the Willis Tower 'Big Willie'...to go with 'Big John', the John Hancock Center, and 'Big Stan', the former Standard Oil Building, a sign that the city may finally be accepting the building's new name. In 2010, the building was renamed the Willis Tower after Willis Group Holdings, a London insurance broker and currently the largest tenant of the tower. The name change will stand for the duration of their ten year lease. Originally, the Willis Tower was called the Sears Tower, after Sears, Roebuck & Company. This company, who commissioned the building as their new headquarters in the early 1970s, played an integral role to the final form and size of the Tower." – Excerpt from a report made by the architectural firm of Skidmore, Owings and Merrill

Over the next several decades, the Sears Tower continued to enjoy its fair share of ups and downs. In 1990, there were rumors flying around that a new firm was going to try to build a taller skyscraper in Chicago, one that would significantly outclass the Tower. Though the plans never got off the ground, J. Paul Beitler, who was behind the scheme, admitted, "We don't believe Sears Tower should stand as man's last triumph in architecture. ... No one knew if a building beyond the height of Sears Tower could be done."

Only a few years passed before the Sears Tower's title of being the tallest building was threatened again. This time, according to the Council on Tall Buildings and Urban Habitat's Height Committee, "The incident that really brought the whole issue of height—and the Council on Tall Buildings and Urban Habitat's Height Committee—to prominence, was the debate in 1996 between Petronas Towers Malaysia and the Sears Tower Chicago. With their decorative spires considered part of the architectural height (similar to the Chrysler Building some 70 years previously), the 452m (1,483ft) Petronas Towers took the title of the world's tallest building away from the then holder Sears Tower by 9.7m (32ft) since the antennae of Sears at 519m (1,704ft) height were not included in its height measurement. However, the twin Petronas Towers were only 379m (1,242ft) without the spires, which was much shorter than both the highest inhabitable floor and flat roof of Sears. Thus viewing the Petronas and Sears Towers side by side (or seeing them in diagrammatic form), it seemed that Sears Tower was much taller, since the two 77m (253 ft) TV antennas brought the total height to 519m (1704ft). At the April 1996 CTBUH Height Committee Meeting, it was decided that the spires should count in the official height of the Petronas Towers, thus giving it the world's tallest title, but it was a decision that many (especially Chicagoans!) disagreed with. Partly in response to this situation, the Council created a further three new height categories: highest occupied floor, highest roof and highest tip of antenna, but this did not necessarily settle the issue, since the architectural height (including spires but not antennae) was the one that determined the world's tallest title. This decision on Petronas versus Sears brought international attention in the news media since this was the first time a country outside the United States had held the world's tallest building. The Sears Tower still held the titles of highest floor (436m/1,431ft) and highest roof (442m/1,451ft), while 1 World Trade Center, New York held the highest antenna title at the time at (527m/1,728ft)."

Not surprisingly, the problem did not stay solved for long. The Committee continued, "Things transitioned again in 2004 with the completion of Taipei 101, Taiwan, which became the world's tallest building at 509m (1,670 ft), beating the Petronas Towers by 57m (187ft). A meeting of the CTBUH Height Committee convened in March that year recognized Taipei 101 with the world's tallest title, along with the highest occupied floor (438m/1,440ft) and highest roof (448m/1,473 ft). There was still some disgruntlement from the US though, as the Sears Tower antennae were still higher than the spires of both Petronas and Taipei 101, at (527m/1730ft—the western antenna had been extended in June 2000 by 8m/26ft)."

By this time, the Sears Tower's owner had other problems to worry about. The dawn of the new millennium brought a marked decline in business for the Sears and Roebuck Company, leading them to downsize the corporate offices and eventually sell the building itself. Graham explained, "They sold the Sears Tower for a huge profit. They made more money selling the building that year, I think, than they made in their whole darn chain of stores. You think they lost money in that building? You've got to be kidding. They made so much money they probably didn't have to pay capital gains taxes, since they were losing a lot in other places."

Like many others, Graham was offended by the sale and the fact that the company Sears sold the building to, the Willis Group, rebranded it the Willis Tower: "A structure of nine bundled tubes, each seventy-five feet square, a very tall building where you can read the spaces in it. There's no reason why it doesn't fit with the others. …was Chartres the same without Chartres Cathedral? I'm not comparing Sears Tower to Chartres, but it made a change. Was Chicago the same before the Palmolive building? A lot of buildings can shape the city. They change it. The facility which we have now to build tall buildings, which we didn't have before, makes it possible to build these buildings economically and therefore not have to use the car so much."

Other citizens were even more upset, and plenty of them vowed never to use the new name. CNN reported in July 2009, "Sears Tower is history. As of Thursday, the iconic Chicago, Illinois, skyscraper is now named Willis Tower. It still looks the same, but Sears Tower in Chicago, Illinois, will have a new name: Willis Tower. At least that's what the owners of the 110-story skyscraper now call it after its new main tenant, the London, England-based insurance broker Willis Group Holdings. However, there are plenty of people who refuse to call it that. More than 90,000 people have joined the group 'People Against the Sears Tower Name Change,' on the social networking Web site Facebook. 'This name change is absurd,' one member wrote. 'Would Paris change the name of the Eiffel Tower? Or London change Buckingham Palace? Or New York, the Statue of Liberty? I believe the Illinois Congress needs to proclaim the Sears Tower a recognizable landmark that is known all over the world by people who have traveled to Chicago.' The group has gathered more than 34,000 signatures on an online petition against the name change. The name change seemed to be a fait accompli, though. A renaming ceremony was scheduled for Thursday with Chicago Mayor Richard Daley. The skyscraper's Web site also features the new name. 'Having our name associated with Chicago's most iconic structure underscores our commitment to this great city, and recognizes Chicago's importance as a major financial hub and international business center,' Willis CEO and Chairman Joseph J. Plumeri said in a news release. The landmark opened in 1973 with its original occupant, Sears Roebuck & Co. The retailing giant has since moved its headquarters to suburban Chicago. That doesn't matter to those against the name change. 'I asked a cabdriver to take me to the Willis tower. He said, 'Where the hell is that?' a member of the Facebook group wrote. 'That pretty much sums it up. No one will start calling it the Willis Tower.'"

In fact, the fight to see the name changed back to Sears Tower continues to this day, with one such call for action reading, "Chicago's iconic Sears Tower has lost its name as part of a deal with London-based insurance broker Willis Group Holdings, Ltd. About 500 employees will be consolidated from Chicago area offices, and the company will occupy about 3.6 percent of the building. We welcome Willis Group Holdings, Ltd., to the Sears Tower and recognize their contribution to the local economy. Their move to the Sears Tower will help to preserve and create jobs, which is especially important for the people of Chicago. While we support their move to the Sears Tower, we do not believe that renaming the building is the proper way to promote their business. Encourage Willis to preserve history and be respectful of the great City of Chicago and its people. Just because the name has changed doesn't mean it can't be changed back."

During this transition period, the Tower went through a number of renovations, one of which added something truly unique to the building. As one article proclaimed in 2009, "The tallest building in North America provides an unrivaled view of a cityscape, all from the comfort of being suspended 1,353 feet in the air. The Sears Tower 'Ledge' has walls, floors, and ceilings made of glass, jutting out from the building to give visitors a unique and vertigo worthy view of Chicago's architectural landscape. The Willis Tower (formerly known as the Sears Tower) is the eleventh tallest building in the world; 110 stories constitute 1,450 feet, making it the tallest building in the Western Hemisphere. The glass boxes, termed 'the Ledges', were opened to the public July 2, 2009. Four 10 foot by 10 foot compartments protrude 4.3 feet from the building's 103rd floor observation room, the Skydeck. With three layers of glass totaling one and a half inches thick, each platform can support up to 5 tons. A completely transparent three sides, top, and bottom designed to generate the sensation of hovering over Chicago do just that, as the box extends far enough for one row of visitors to stand suspended at a time. A clear day presents a view of up to 50 miles and four states. Structural glass design experts of Halcrow Yolles took the original architectural plans (firm Skidmore, Owings and Merril) a step further, from the concept of devising a retractable structure for easy cleaning, to detailing each box to have near-invisible structural support. All the side and bottom perimeter steel was removed, completing the floating on air appearance. The idea for the Ledges supposedly originated from the constant cleaning workers had to do on the Skydeck's windows. Tourists every day would press their foreheads against the glass, attempting to peer down at the city, leaving smudges that were becoming tiring to clean. Now the staff will need to clean the occasional footprint left by fearless children, or handprints from nervous guests ensuring the walls are still there."

Dan Schwen's picture of the glass balconies on the side of the 103rd floor

Mike Gonzalez's picture of one of the glass balconies

2009 also saw the Tower become part of the "Go Green" movement as "officials announced a $350 million 5-year green renovation plan that includes the installation of wind turbines, roof gardens, and solar panels." The *New York Times* reported, "The Sears Tower, that bronze-black monument that forms the 110-story peak of the skyline here and stands as the tallest office building in the Western Hemisphere, will soon have another unique feature: wind turbines sprouting from its recessed rooftops high in the sky. The building's owners, leasing agents and architects said Wednesday that they are literally taking environmental sustainability to new heights with a $350 million retrofit of the 1970s-era modernist building — and the turbines are only the tip of the transformation. The plan, to begin immediately, aims to reduce electricity use in the tower by 80 percent over five years through upgrades in the glass exterior, internal lighting, heating, cooling and elevator systems — and its own green power generation. In such a huge tower, with 4.5 million square feet of office and retail space, 16,000 windows and 104 elevators, the project is bound to be one of the most substantial green renovations ever tried on one site, planners said. The Sears Tower is significantly larger than the 102-story, 2.6-million-square-foot Empire State Building, for instance, which is also undergoing renovation to reduce energy consumption."

Commenting on the changes, architect Adrian Smith, who helped design the improvements, observed, "If we can take care of one building that size, it has a huge impact on society. It is a village in and of itself." The *Times* article went on to provide further details: "Buildings are among the world's largest contributors of greenhouse gas emissions. After the retrofit, energy savings at the Sears Tower, which is to be renamed the Willis Tower this summer, would be equal to 150,000 barrels of oil a year, officials said. The savings are expected to help redeem some of the project's cost, which is to be financed through private equity investment, grants, debt financing and government funds. The Sears Tower plans to open a first-floor center to educate the public about the redesign, and hopes to serve as a model for other aging skyscrapers around the world, officials said."

Eventually, the Sears Tower lost its title in 2010 when construction was completed on the Burj Khalifa in the United Arab Emirates. According to SOM, who designed the world's tallest building in Dubai, "The design for the 162-story tower combines local cultural influences with cutting-edge technology to achieve high performance in an extreme desert climate. The centerpiece of a large mixed-use development, the Burj Khalifa contains offices, retail space, residential units, and a Giorgio Armani hotel. A Y-shaped floor plan maximizes views of the Arabian Gulf. At ground level, the skyscraper is surrounded by green space, water features, and pedestrian-friendly boulevards. The tower's overall design was inspired by the geometries of a regional desert flower and the patterning systems embodied in Islamic architecture. Built of reinforced concrete and clad in glass, the tower is composed of sculpted volumes arranged around a central buttressed core. As the tower rises from a flat base, setbacks occur in an upward spiraling pattern, reducing the building's mass as it reaches skyward. At the pinnacle, the central core emerges and forms a spire."

Regardless, the Willis Tower remains one of the tallest building in the Western Hemisphere, and it is still the tallest skyscraper built before 2000. This remains a source of pride for both those who built it and the people of Chicago as a whole. Looking back across the decades, Graham summed up his experience with the Sears Tower by saying, "At the beginning of SOM, when I was there, none of us would take credit for the building. We refused to do that. But finally, people started to push. Architects were bowing even when bows were not required. So finally, SOM changed the policy…The managing partner for the project, the design partner for the project, the engineers, the project managers—we listed them all. ... There isn't a chief. There isn't one guy.... There's a partners committee and a chairman. ... I called myself 'janitor of the committee.' ... It was a more intimate relationship with clients. You just cannot go around and do big projects and say, 'Well, I did it all.' That's baloney! Absolute baloney. Impossible!"

Bibliography

Billington, David. *The Tower and the Bridge: The New Art of Structural Engineering.* Princeton University Press. (1985)

Pridmore, Jay. *Sears Tower: A Building Book.* Chicago Architecture Foundation. (2002)

Tamboli, Akbar. *Tall and Super Tall Buildings: Planning and Design.* McGraw-Hill Professional (2014)

Made in the USA
Monee, IL
05 December 2020

51054307R00028